# SCOTT JOPLIN
## PIANO RAGS
### BOOK ONE

PAXTON

# SCOTT JOPLIN AND HIS MUSIC

Scott Joplin was born into a poor negro family in Texas in 1868—just three years after the abolition of slavery in the United States. By the time he was ten years old his self-taught piano-playing was skilful enough to attract attention, and he was brought to a local white teacher to acquire the rudiments of a musical education. In his teens he left home to earn a living as a saloon pianist in St Louis; he played cornet in a brass band for a period, and also organized a vocal group, at the same time continuing with studies in harmony and composition.

St Louis, a bustling cosmopolitan port on the Mississippi, was the birthplace of the new negro art of Ragtime, the exuberant piano-style which had developed from the mildly-syncopated minstrel songs and dances. Among many talented negro pianists and entertainers, Scott Joplin was the first with the ability to set down in musical notation the new rhythms, and melodies played off-the-beat.

His second published rag, *Maple Leaf*, swept the country in 1899 as a nationwide hit, and remains the most famous ragtime number; its success enabled Joplin to retire from public performance and devote himself to composition. He was already accepted as the leading Ragtime composer, and a steady development is shown in the string of rags he produced over the next ten years.

The early Joplin compositions contain elements familiar among the creative ragtime professors: many strongly rhythmic strains built from reiterated syncopations, as in *Maple Leaf Rag* and the driving last strain of *Elite Syncopations*; and many other liltingly tuneful strains developed from the cake-walk and from negro folk-lore, as in *The Entertainer* and *The Ragtime Dance* (which was first published as a song-and-dance number). In his later work we see the development of a wholly personal style, with a gentle melancholy in the graceful themes that are overlaid on the jaunty ragtime rhythms. These mature compositions are well represented in the present two albums, including *Rose Leaf Rag* (a worthy counterpart to the early *Maple Leaf*); the complex *Euphonic Sounds*; and *Solace*, his most personal statement of all, where the steady onward rhythm is broken by emotionally-charged pauses.

The final period of advanced rags, experimental both in rhythm and harmony, with many strains in minor keys, is represented by *Scott Joplin's New Rag* and *Magnetic Rag*.

Joplin also published waltzes, songs and marches, and increasingly concentrated his efforts on his ambitions to become an operatic composer. He lived to see the formal intricacies of piano ragtime lose favour before the new craze for the jazz bands, and died in 1917 in a mental hospital, his mind broken after the failure to secure a hearing for the ragtime opera *Treemonisha* to which he had devoted so many years work.

*Charles Wilford*
*May 1974*

# CONTENTS

The pieces in this album will be found on
Joshua Rifkin's recording, *Piano Rags by
Scott Joplin*, issued by Nonesuch Records
as an L.P. (H-71248), a cassette (ZCH-71248),
and a cartridge (Y8H-71248).

# MAPLE LEAF RAG

Tempo di marcia

TRIO

# THE ENTERTAINER
## A Ragtime Two Step

Repeat 8va

# RAGTIME DANCE
## A Stop Time Two Step

**Not too fast**

NOTICE: To get the desired effect of 'Stop Time', the pianist will please <u>Stamp</u> the heel of one foot heavily upon the floor at the word 'Stamp'. Do not raise the toe from the floor while <u>stamping</u>.

*Stamp*        *Stamp*        *Stamp*        *Stamp*        *Stamp*        *Stamp*        *Stamp*        *Stamp*

# GLADIOLUS RAG

Note: Do not play this piece fast.
It is never right to play 'Ragtime' fast.
*Composer*

**Slow march tempo**

# FIG LEAF RAG

# SCOTT JOPLIN'S NEW RAG

Allegro moderato

CODA

FINE

# EUPHONIC SOUNDS
## A Syncopated Two Step

Note: Do not play this piece fast.
It is never right to play 'Ragtime' fast.
*Composer*

**Slow March time**

FINE

# MAGNETIC RAG

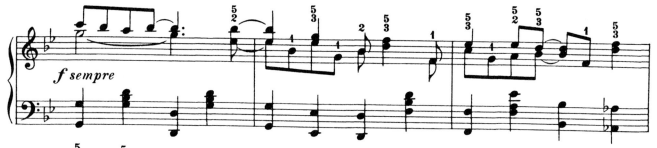

Tempo l'istesso

Published by Paxton Music Limited